ELEMENTARY TEACHER EDUCATION IN KOREA

Phi Delta Kappa
International Studies in Education

We can only see in a picture what our experience
permits us to see.

Edgar Dale

The Phi Delta Kappa International Studies in Education Series was established as a way to enlarge the common experience of education by publishing studies that bring to readers knowledge of heretofore unfamiliar theories, philosophies, and practices in the profession of education.

As the interdependence of nations becomes increasingly evident and necessary with the passage of time, so too must our understandings about education become shared property. In thus sharing, we come increasingly to comprehend one another across civilizations and cultures, for education is at the core of human endeavor. Through education we pass on to succeeding generations not merely the accumulated wisdom of our past but the vision and means to create the future.

Elementary Teacher Education in Korea is the first monograph in this series.

INTERNATIONAL STUDIES IN EDUCATION

ELEMENTARY
TEACHER
EDUCATION
IN KOREA

by Douglas C. Smith

PHI DELTA KAPPA
EDUCATIONAL FOUNDATION
Bloomington, Indiana

Cover design by
Peg Caudell

Library of Congress Catalog Card Number 94-65001
ISBN 0-87367-465-0
Copyright © 1994 by the Phi Delta Kappa Educational Foundation
Bloomington, Indiana

To my mother,
Jane Anderson Smith Engel

ACKNOWLEDGMENTS

This study of Korean teacher education owes its existence to the Korea Foundation of Seoul, which in 1992 awarded me a generous grant to do field research on the peninsular republic and the South Korean island of Cheju. I am honored also to have been named a Fellow of this distinguished foundation.

Many Americans and Koreans helped me with travel, research, and writing and with understanding Korean society, culture, and education. To all, I acknowledge my deep-felt indebtedness.

As in the past with my other books and articles (dating from 1976), Mrs. Grace L. Henderson contributed significantly to the readability of this work. Her jeweler's eye spotted errors and omissions, and her good sense made this work much better than it otherwise might have been.

In Korea, three associates willingly helped me with my understanding, research, itinerary, and travel: Ms. Kim Ok-jin, Ms. Yoon Keun-jin, and Ms. Lee Young-mee. Ms. Judi Strider Fadeley did her usual splendid job of typing the manuscript from my convoluted handwriting; and Ms. Cassandra Wheeler helped with the bibliography.

Dr. John R. Diebolt, Dr. Virginia Richmond, and Provost William Vehse, all at West Virginia University, gave me the necessary support and encouragement to complete the field research, as did Dr. Bruce Clayton Flack, director of Academic Affairs for Higher Education in West Virginia. Personnel at the Shepherd College Library assisted with gathering materials from the Library of Congress and ERIC.

I am indebted to many Korean scholars, professors, administrators, college and university presidents, school teachers, students, medical doctors, business persons, embassy personnel, Ministry of Education staff, and Westerners living in Korea for their insights into Korean education, society, religion, language, economics, foreign and domestic military policy, teachers' lives, architecture, music and art, culture and cuisine. I conducted 53 interviews while I was in Korea in 1992. To the fine and generous women and men who spent untold hours with me, I extend my deepest thanks and hope especially that this work reflects correctly the realities of their nation's teacher education system.

Douglas C. Smith, Ph.D., Litt.D.
Shepherdstown, West Virginia

TABLE OF CONTENTS

INTRODUCTION

*The Nobility, and all Free-men in general, take great care of the
Education of their children, and put them very young to learn to Read
and Write, to which that Nation is much addicted.*

Hendrik Hamel, the first Westerner to live in Korea,
writing in 1667 in his *Journal*

I had the good fortune to be the first West Virginian to be awarded 'Fellow' status in the Korea Foundation. This honor was accompanied by a generous grant to do field research in Korea on teacher education and related facets of Korean civilization that have affected educational vitality. As used in this monograph, Korea refers to only the Republic of Korea, or South Korea.

Modern Korea is a highly developed industrial, technical, consumer-oriented society. Good public transportation, historic palaces and museums, and modern skyscrapers are found in the urban and suburban areas. Cafés and restaurants serving foods from all around the world, as well Korean cuisine, can be found even in the smallest cities. Recreational facilities, churches and temples, and parks are available to all the people of this modern entrepreneurial society. Korea is much like America or Japan in its level of health care, life expectancy, dietary intake, and technological and artistic advancement.

On any given day, children and adolescents can be seen riding buses to and from school, their arms loaded with books. On sunny days at historic sites, students can be found painting and drawing on large pads of paper. Korea has been one of the most successful nations on earth in the production of educators and highly motivated students. Achievement scores of Korean children are currently the highest of all the developed countries (UNESCO 1990). Many features of Korean society contribute to this standing. The selection, preparation, and education of elementary school teachers is one important ingredient in the high level of school success that students enjoy in the Republic of Korea.

Prior to embarking on this research project, I reviewed the literature currently available (in English) on the Korean model of teacher education. My focus during the field research was on the methods used to prepare teachers for Korea's elementary schools. The general goals that I laid out for myself were:

3

- to become better informed about the historical roots of teacher education in Korea,
- to investigate the relationship between Korean culture and history and the place of the teacher in Korean society,
- to understand Korean teacher education in comparison to teacher education in the United States, and
- to open channels of communication and to develop relationships with Korean scholars interested in comparative teacher education.

My methodology specifically required that I explore the following topics in depth:

- philosophical bases for teacher education in Korea,
- how students are admitted to teacher colleges,
- socioeconomic status of prospective teachers,
- models for teacher training at different postsecondary levels,
- teacher-in-training internships,
- administrative forms in the various teacher-training institutions,
- job placement of new teachers and teacher dismissal,
- certification and inservice training,
- government-university relations as applied to teacher training, and
- the relationship between the teacher education curriculum and national objectives.

While in Korea, I visited 10 colleges and universities. I interviewed 53 persons, including college presidents, deans, professors, instructors, graduate students, undergraduates, school teachers, school principals, physicians, government officials, Westerners living and working in Korea, business persons, and others, many of whom owe their personal success to the Korean system of education. In conjunction with interviews, I also was invited to speak to students, to visit libraries, and to interact with college and university professors in informal settings.

Research materials were supplied to me by colleges, the Ministry of Education, the Korea Research Foundation, the Korea Cultural and Arts Foundation, the Korean Education Development Institute, the United States Information Service, and the Korean Embassy in Washington, D.C. A total of 60 pounds of documents, books, articles, and other printed materials accompanied me home.

The entire subject of comparative teacher education research is in its infancy. The specific field of assessment and description of another

4

society's elementary teacher education system is virtually nonexistent in the literature of cross-cultural research.

In preparing this monograph, a conscious effort has been made to describe the preservice education of teachers in Korea and to relate other aspects of Korean society that have contributed to the uniqueness of this educative process. An equally powerful concern was to do this without drawing critical comparisons to other nations' education paradigms. Each civilization has developed in its own ways of educating future teachers. For an American to visit another society and pass judgment on that society's social, political, economic, or education system — without a detailed and thorough understanding of the evolution of the civilization — would be to commit academic sophistry. Consequently, this monograph is devoted primarily to describing Korean elementary teacher education.

Projects like this one can take several different forms: 1) the research report, 2) the evaluative study, and 3) the essay. *Research* in this context means "careful, critical, disciplined inquiry, varying in technique and method according to the nature of the problem identified, directed toward the clarification or resolution (or both) of the problem." *Evaluation* refers to "judgments of merit, sometimes based solely on measurements such as those provided by test scores, but more frequently involving the synthesis of various measurements, critical incidents, subjective impressions, and other kinds of evidence weighed in the process of carefully appraising the effects of an educational experience" (*Dictionary of Education* 1973, p. 494).

An *essay*, according to my *Webster's*, is "an analytic or interpretive written literary work dealing with a subject from a limited or personal point of view; an effort to examine or assay various components or characteristics of that which is under study; an initial tentative effort." Although this monograph is a composite of the three vehicles defined above, I have attempted to emphasize the last, the essay. As a "tentative effort" at describing Korean teacher education, I have felt free to take certain liberties with style, methodology, and format. This informality should not diminish the validity of the information but, I hope, will allow for greater accessibility to the ideas and philosophies discussed.

J.R. Kidd indicated that there are certain goals that must be kept in the forefront when one is involved with trans-social comparative education studies. Though Kidd used these propositions in relation to comparative adult education, they are equally applicable to the study of another society's teacher education programs. These goals are:

- to enhance further understanding and communication between two societies,
- to become better informed about the education system for pedagogues of other countries,
- to become better informed about the ways in which people in other cultures have carried out certain social functions by means of education,
- to become better informed about the historical roots of certain activities and thus to develop criteria for assessing contemporary developments and testing possible outcomes,
- to understand better the educational forms and systems operating in one's own country,
- to satisfy an interest in how other human beings live and learn,
- to understand oneself better, and
- to reveal how one's own cultural biases and personal attributes affect one's judgment about possible ways of carrying on learning transactions (Kidd 1981, p. 220).

These goals form the focus for the information that follows. Each section moves from the general to the specific. I have attempted, first, to introduce readers to cultural, social, and institutional attributes of Korea and then to discuss the specifics of the educative process as a reflection of these attributes.

In all societies, teacher education is both a product and a transmitter of cultural values. In my research, I explored both the activities that are carried out in Korea's colleges of education and the ensuing relationships between teacher training, cultural development, and respect for education. I also examined the concept of melding pedagogy and ethical development for young people.

British writer H.G. Wells said that the future history of humans would be a race between education and destruction. That his prediction could be true is becoming increasingly evident on a global scale. Only a truly well-educated citizenry can think logically, act sensibly, respect freedom, and work toward the betterment of its society. Education is the vehicle that precludes civilization's decline.

Teacher education symbolizes the vitality of a nation. Indifference to schools and teachers may betoken general anti-intellectualism in the nation's leadership. Rigidly authoritarian classrooms and teaching techniques suggest totalitarianism, as is found in Communist countries. Poor use of teachers' time and educational resources may be an extension of the inability of government and society to effectively use the resources at their disposal. And if teacher education is seen as inferior to traditional college study, then the quality of those choosing pedagogy as a profession may suffer.

I began writing this monograph shortly after returning from my Korea sojourn in November 1992. Almost 10 years earlier, in April 1983, the National Commission on Excellence in Education, chaired by Dr. Terrel Bell, then Secretary of Education under President Ronald Reagan, had published *A Nation at Risk: The Imperative for Educational Reform*. I still retain the copy of this important document that was sent to me by Senator Robert C. Byrd. *A Nation at Risk* suggested that America was falling far behind other less prosperous but seemingly more determined nations in preparing teachers and youngsters for their place in society. The Commission rang a note of alarm when it stated:

> If an unfriendly foreign power had attempted to impose on America the mediocre educational performance that exists today, we might have viewed it as an act of war. As it stands, we have allowed this to happen to ourselves. We have even squandered the gains in student achievement made in the wake of the Sputnik challenge. Moreover, we have dismantled essential [teacher education] support systems which helped make those gains possible. We have, in effect, been committing an act of unthinkable, unilateral educational disarmament. (1983, p. 1)

Teachers in the United States, the report concluded, were poorly prepared in subject matter, were drawn from the lower part of both the high school and college graduating classes, tended to take soft "educational methods" courses in lieu of the more rigorous subjects, were paid far too little for the duties they perform, and often were assigned to teach out of their subject field. The report suggested that in the most critical fields of learning — mathematics, computers, foreign languages, and physical and biological sciences — a dire shortage of qualified elementary and secondary teachers existed.

This monograph focuses on how another society today is attempting to deal with many of the concerns raised a decade ago in *A Nation at Risk*. To the best of my knowledge, no systematic effort (in the English language) has been made to study the unique and successful model of teacher education that exists in modern Korea.

The purpose of this type of project is not to find fault with an education system, but rather to learn from a comparative assessment about another society's institutions and then to use this knowledge to bridge the knowledge gap between American and Korean education. I also had as a parallel purpose to discover ways that American elementary teacher education and, consequently, public school education in general might be improved.

As the United States continues to address reform in American education, I am hopeful that educators, parents, and concerned citizens will be willing to see societies like Korea not as potential competitors, but as laboratories where experiments in educational excellence are taking place and as societies from which America can learn. It is through comparative studies, such as this one, that we can better understand American education by reflecting on our own society from the vantage point of another culture.

ORIENTATIONS

The Confucian educational tradition has provided Koreans with a reasonable way of thinking, a strong moral sense, and a zeal for education of stressing that man can be a man only through education.
Dr. Park Sun-young in *Koreana*, 1991

Korea is a peninsular nation. Understanding this geographic factor is necessary to understanding this beautiful, important, sophisticated, and enduring civilization.

Korea's neighbors have received so much attention in recent years that Korea often has been overlooked in the process. China, with its splendid past, vast land mass, and huge population, and Japan, which has played a major role in world history since the late 19th century, have both dominated and overshadowed Korea to such a degree that few Western scholars have chosen to examine Korean society, history, or education. As a consequence, Korea has been relegated to second-class status by scholars of Asian studies. China and Japan simply are too attractive and too available for most Western scholars who wish to research the East. Yet a review of Korean history and culture suggests that the country is a major developer and transmitter of civilization and has played a decisive role in Asian affairs.

Located in the eastern part of the North Asian Continent, the Korean peninsula seems to jut out of China at the place where the Yalu River separates most of Asia from the peninsular nation. To its west, Korea faces northern China across the Yellow Sea. To the east, Korea is surrounded by the Japanese islands across the East Sea (also called the Sea of Japan). The South Sea encircles the southern coast of the peninsula. Four distinct seasons divide the year, with very hot, humid summers and below-freezing winters being common. The ideal season to visit Korea is autumn, when the weather is dry and sunny and the temperature is moderate.

Most of the population in South Korea (45 million in 1992) live in and near its major cities. Seoul, the capital, has a population in excess of 10 million. The land is characterized by high mountains in the east and lower hills and plains in the west. Few forests remain in Korea; farming and fishing are major industries. The total land size of Korea about equals that of Minnesota. Topographically the

11

peninsula is not dissimilar to West Virginia, with extensive mountain ranges and scattered pockets of population. Beautiful islets surround the peninsula, the largest being Cheju, about 100 miles off the southern coast. During my sojourn in Korea in 1992, I spent a week on this island province, called Cheju-do. My main purpose was to do research at the National Cheju Teachers College and Cheju University, both of which are located in the island's provincial seat, also called Cheju.

Cheju is the largest of the hundreds of islands that surround the peninsula. The island (about 700 square miles) lies approximately 250 miles south of Seoul and 110 miles south of the peninsula's major coastal city of Pusan. It is one of the eleven provinces (states) that form the Republic of Korea. At its the center rises Halla-san, 6,000 feet above sea level. Halla-san was an active volcano until rather recently. It last erupted in the 14th century. Climbers now scale its height routinely; the seven-hour trek is a strenuous workout. Those who brave the climb are rewarded with a spectacular view across a mile-wide crystal-clear lake that fills the volcano's mouth.

Cheju was the last stronghold of the Mongolian empire, which occupied most of Asia and much of eastern Europe under the Yuan Dynasty (A.D. 1231-1392). Horse stock that was brought to Cheju by the Mongolians remains an important part of the economy. Fishing, farming, coral gathering, and tourism are also important in the island's diverse economy. Cheju island differs from the peninsula in a number of ways, but perhaps most significant is that island society is matriarchal. Women do most of the labor and take care of all money matters; men oversee home life and child care.

The climate of the island is milder than on the Korean peninsula, but the winters can be very windy and brisk. Home and farm design reflects this unusual climate. Stone walls and thatch-roofed cottages are common. Cheju is a favorite vacation place for the people of Korea.

A Culture of Traditions

Most of the cultural attributes of Korea have their provenance in Chinese civilization; Confucianism is an example. The Korean academic community is quick to acknowledge the importance of China in the evolution of the peninsula. Until quite recently, education in Korea was modeled on the traditional Chinese system, as was the structure of the government. Confucian classics and periodic examinations were the leitmotif of the enduring education model. Japan also was the beneficiary of other nations' cultural, artistic, linguistic, and educational heritage. China transferred its institutions to the peoples of Chosŏn (pronounced *chō-sŏn*, a name used for Korea since the second millennium B.C.). Korea, in turn, became the main transmitter of civilization to its neighbor, Japan. However, Japanese scholars seem reluctant to acknowledge the role Korea and its people (many of whom held major jobs in Japan's government during the Shogun and Chosŏn eras) played in bringing culture and development to the Land of the Rising Sun. Public school texts in Japan tend not to credit Korea's many contributions, although Japan does acknowledge its Chinese legacy.

The earliest ancestors to modern-day Koreans entered the peninsula at least five thousand years ago. Three Korean kingdoms emerged in Korea's early history — Koguryŏ, Paekche, and Silla. By A.D. 668, Silla (with Chinese support) had conquered the other nation-states. This unification usually is regarded as the formation of the Korean state. Silla gave way to Koryŏ in 936, and Koryŏ to the Yi Dynasty in 1392. The Yi Dynasty, which brought the establishment of a Confucian state, was to endure more than 500 years, until Japan occupied Korea in 1910. The conquest of Korea lasted until the end of World War II, when outside control of Korea passed into the hands of the Western democracies and the Soviet Union. Not until the conclusion of the Korean War in 1953 and the division of the peninsula at the 38th parallel was the Republic of Korea in the south able to construct an orderly education system that now is recognized as one of the best in the world.

Many features of modern-day Korea make this peninsular civilization unique. Perhaps the most profound feature is the homogeneity of the Korean populace. Virtually all Korean citizens share a common ancestry that stretches back 3,000 to 5,000 years. Unlike the great civilizations of the West, which have gained sustenance from immigrants bringing cultural and religious attributes with them, Korea has built its civilization, language, cultural heritage, political institutions, financial system, and education paradigm on a homogeneous polity. Even Japan and Taiwan, which we think of as ethnologically pure, have far more foreigners living in their societies.

The disadvantage of a monocultural civilization is that new ideas and styles of living must be transplanted or copied from other Asian and Western nations. The advantage is that certain assumptions can be made, the main one being that all members of the society have similar childhood and adolescent experiences, attend schools that are essentially identical, speak the same language with equal ability, and hold many of the same aspirations for their lives and the lives of their children.

The Korean language is one of the most sophisticated and scientific on earth. Dr. Hong Say-myung of the Korea Research Foundation states:

> Koreans speak a common tongue that is more like Turkic, Finnish, or Hungarian than like other Asian languages. Until the end of the 15th century, Koreans had used Chinese characters for writing. Then an enlightened monarch, Sejong the Great (1399-1450), appointed a royal commission which devised an efficient system of phonetic alphabet called "Hangul." The simplicity and practicality of Hangul has permitted Koreans in modern times to achieve a literacy level that exceeds 95 percent.
>
> Korean is a complex language. First, it is built up of Korean words and Chinese equivalents. The Chinese derivatives are used in speech and writing. Second, the language reflects levels of society by the use of different vocabulary and grammatical endings. The relative degree of intimacy or familiarity between people is clearly reflected in the language forms. By changing the verb endings, many of the niceties of relationships are clearly expressed (Hong 1989, p. 142).

Educational Foundations

Korean education, based on long-standing historical precedents, in many respects has changed relatively little in two thousand years. Of all the institutions in Korea, three have functioned as the ballast for this civilization: the family, religious beliefs, and a strong desire for education.

While we in the West have garnered our ethical and moral sustenance from Christianity, the Koreans have relied on education as the vehicle for upward mobility, good government, social and political harmony, and a general absence of societal rancor. When our ancestors were carving up Europe (and each other) over territoriality, Korea under the Yi Dynasty (1392-1910) established a strong centralized government with efficient administrative systems, regional transportation, printing with movable type, and a body of educational ideals that even today are a model for developing nations.

The Korean word for teacher, *san sun nim*, can be used to help focus on what the teaching-learning process means in Korea. The compound — which is three characters — shows how deeply rooted in Korean cultural activity the educative system remains. The characters collectively mean "to guide, counsel, teach, educate" and denote a high moral bearing for the person who is called "teacher."

The education process in both learning and pedagogy is viewed as a two-fold activity. First is the transmission of knowledge from one generation to the next. The concept of developing new ideas through a thorough understanding of the old is embedded in this transmission. Hence, to be fully educated, one must first acquire knowledge and understanding of that which has already been accepted.

Second, and perhaps more important, is the view that the school, whether for three-year-olds or postdoctoral students, is where values, morals, and ethical priorities will be learned. Seen as more than a transmitter of information, the traditional and modern teacher in Korea is responsible for shaping the moral and ethical views of students, first, by his or her personal behavior and, second, by what he or she demands of students.

While American teachers are constrained to be relatively neutral on topics of an ethical nature, the Koreans instill in their teachers the idea that they are examples for their students and that ideas expressed in classes and behaviors exhibited in public function as models for future generations and the society in general. To bring moral arguments into the classroom is unacceptable in modern Western pedagogy; in Korea it is expected that the teacher, whether in the elementary school or at an elite university, will constantly evaluate his or her behavior, lectures, and responses on both cognitive and ethical levels.

All societies set certain goals for their education systems. The goals of modern Korean education, in the broadest sense, are to bring about personal enrichment and development, to engender social harmony, and to build a cadre of skilled men and women who can answer the challenges of their nation's industrial growth, population problems, land and sea usage, and political and diplomatic activities. Political indoctrination is not an overt component of the education process.

The goals of a nation's education system cannot be easily separated from the historical evolution that has brought the society to its current form. Some of the goals of today's Korean education are found in all civilized nations; others are unique to the peninsular state. All the values that an education system attempts to perpetuate through its formal and informal settings must be synergistic with the general social, political, and economic aims that both the extrinsic government policy dictates and the intrinsic historical evolutionary process has left as its legacy.

The schools of modern Korea are government-controlled or government-sanctioned institutions that are charged to develop mores, attitudes, skills, behavior patterns, and a future-orientedness that will allow a majority of their students to find both a worthy place in the society and personal meaning in their lives. Because of the homogeneity of the Korean population, few conflicts exist between the goals of schools and the values found in peer-group relationships, family life, religious institutions, or government, military, or business enterprises.

Korean education focuses on ensuring the orderly transmission of the national heritage and developing attitudes that reinforce the importance of "the group" — family, siblings, peers, community, nation — in harmonious and prosperous living. Education, suggests Ronald S. Anderson in *Comparative Educational Systems*:

> has to answer at least three different kinds of demands: (1) the demand of the state which as part of the national investment requires a pool of the labor force with highly developed skills enabling the state to advance economically and become modernized; (2) the demand of the individual as a consumer of education for the development of personal potential and for preparation for a career, as well as for education as an end itself, for the individual's own enjoyment — this latter is possible only when the society has become more affluent; and (3) the demand inherent in social change, the extension of equality of opportunity as a way of extending democracy. (Ignas 1981, pp. 233-34)

The Law and Education

The specific aims of Korean education are found in the Charter of National Education and the Korean Constitution. With the acceleration of modernization during the 1960s, pursuit of change and progress at the expense of traditional values became a dominant theme in Korean life. The country already had witnessed a disruption of old ways and customs caused by the massive influx of Western culture and technology. Such discontinuity of tradition brought about much confusion in the general value system. Thus it became necessary for national leaders to define a philosophical background for national endeavors related to modernization and to reinstate the traditional values as worthwhile resources of wisdom and knowledge for modern times. It was in this social context that efforts were made to redefine the ideals and goals of education in the form of the Charter of National Education, proclaimed in 1968.

16

Subsequently, Article 31 of the Constitution, promulgated in 1983, mandated:

1. All citizens shall have the right to receive equal education according to their ability.
2. All citizens shall have the duty of ensuring that all children within their protection receive an elementary education, and that this education is regulated by law.
3. Compulsory education shall be free.
4. Independence, professionalism, political impartiality, and college autonomy in education shall be guaranteed in accordance with the law.
5. The state shall promote lifelong education.
6. Fundamental matters pertaining to the education system, including in-school and lifelong education, administration, finance, and the status of teachers, shall be determined by law.

The basic directions and objectives of education are spelled out according to these provisions in the Education Law. Section I of this law provides the following general rules:

Article 1: Education shall, under the great ideal of *hongik-ingan* (benefits for mankind — the founding spirit of the first kingdom in Korean history), aim to assist all people in perfecting their individual character, developing the ability for an independent life, and acquiring the qualifications of citizens capable of participating in the building of a democratic state and promoting the prosperity of all human mankind.

Article 2: In order to achieve these aims, the following educational objectives shall be set up:
   a. Development of the knowledge and attitudes needed for a sound cultivation and sustenance of health and the cultivation of an indomitable spirit.
   b. Development of a patriotic spirit for the preservation of national independence and enhancement of an ideal for the cause of world peace.
   c. Transmission and development of national culture and its contribution to the creation and growth of world civilization.
   d. Fostering of a truth-seeking spirit and the ability of scientific thinking for creative activity and rational living.
   e. Development of a love for freedom and of respect for responsibility necessary to lead a well-harmonized community

life with the spirit of faithfulness, cooperation and understanding.

f. Development of an aesthetic sensibility to create and ap-
preciate arts, enjoy the beauty of nature, and utilize lei-
sure effectively for a joyful wholesome life.

g. Cultivation of industriousness and dedication to one's work
in order to become a competent producer and wise
consumer.

Article 8 stipulates the right to receive basic education by stating:
"Every person shall be entitled to receive an elementary education
of six years."

Modern Compulsory Education

Today Korean education shares many characteristics found in other
developed nations. Leaders of the various institutions and those in
government positions, in large part, have been influenced by the con-
figuration of U.S. education. There are differences between Korean
and U.S. education, but the differences are more process than in-
tent. The objective of education in Korea and the rest of the developed world remains constant — to encourage a sense of self-worth
in students, to pass on the heritage and goals of the nation, and to
create an educated citizenry that will continue the development of
the civilization.

One major process difference is the high degree of national government involvement in Korean education. In the United States there
is no nationwide system of schools under a central authority. There
is no formal national curriculum or national system of education
finance, teacher certification, graduation standards, or professional
ethics. Rather, state and local control result in a wide diversity in
schools, their curricula, and the standards by which they function.
By contrast, centralization characterizes the administrative structure
of Korean education. One governing body — the Ministry of Education — administers all public higher education, teacher preservice
training, and international education and exchange programs. Many
private colleges and universities exist in Korea, but they also must
abide by Ministry of Education directives and regulations.

At the first level of education is the national compulsory system,
which includes grades one to nine. (Kindergarten is not compulsory, although there are more than 8,000 kindergartens, many privately
operated, enrolling some 415,000 pupils.) Until 1969, compulsory

18

education ended after sixth grade; and an examination was required to matriculate into junior high school. Then the pressures of economic growth and the need for a more highly skilled work force caused the government to increase the length of compulsory education to nine years. This decision was important to the evolution of the pedagogical processes in Korea, because more teachers, facilities, administrators, and funds were needed to effect this change. With the type of centralized education administration that exists in Korea, the process of upgrading compulsory education from six to nine years was accomplished with a minimum of rancor.

Today approximately 99% of Korean children between the ages of 6 and 15 attend a public or a private school or are in a special education facility. In 1992 there were 6,400 elementary schools with a total enrollment of 4,900,000. There were 2,500 open and free junior high schools with a student population of 2,280,000.

Supplemental and special education for blind, deaf, physically handicapped, and retarded youngsters is not a major dimension of the education structure in South Korea. Gifted education programs in the regular school setting and mainstreaming children with mild handicaps are the current policies. American educators have served as consultants in the field of special education and, in fact, most special education programs were started by American missionaries.

The next level of the education system in Korea is the secondary school. Secondary schools include academic high schools and senior vocational schools. Movement from the ninth grade to public or private high schools is determined by a national examination.

The goal of the academic high school is to prepare young men and women (ages 15 to 18) in subject matter that will have a direct bearing on their college and university education. Although only 35% of those admitted to academic high schools are able to pass the required university entrance examination and thus matriculate to a college or university, these schools have as their mission to prepare all who attend in academic subjects. Currently, some 1.5 million students attend academic high schools; and tremendous pressure is placed on students to be admitted to an academic high school. The number of these schools has increased in the last 40 years, but the number of students has increased disproportionately to the real population growth. This imbalance suggests both greater affluence and the recognition that advanced education is the means of achieving affluence. A major complaint heard in Korea is that the academic high school teaches children how to pass the national competitive examination and not how to prepare for the vicissitudes of life in a dynamic society and changing world.

Korea also is working to improve its vocational secondary schools and to increase the number of these schools. The thirst for technical training is strong among those who choose not to go to the academic high school. There are some 597 vocational secondary schools with nearly 811,000 students. Virtually any socially relevant vocational, technical, or industrial subject can be studied, including agricultural science, fishery studies, commerce, home economics, nursing, and other fields. A competitive examination also is required for admission to a vocational-technical institution. These schools are evenly distributed throughout Korea, and eventually about 65% of all high school students will find their way into one of these settings.

Higher Education and Lifelong Learning

Higher education in modern Korea comprises professional junior colleges, four-year degree-granting colleges, universities, and research centers. Korea has numerous universities and 11 four-year teachers colleges. (A college may become a university when it has master's degree programs and meets specific criteria of the Ministry of Education.) Korea has 511 institutions of higher learning with a total student population of 1.4 million.

Graduate education also has become an important part of education in Korea. Two years beyond the B.A. normally are required to earn the master's degree. The Ph.D. normally is awarded after three to five years of further study. Part-time and evening education at the graduate level currently are available.

Students may earn a bachelor's degree by attending five years of evening education. The requirements for the four-year day B.A. and five-year night-school degree are essentially the same, although the day student appears to have more prestige in Korean society. Professional fields require differing lengths of time for completing a degree. For example, law and architecture require five years; dentistry, six years; and medicine, seven to nine years of study. The Ph.D. degree may take up to 10 years to complete.

Adult lifelong education makes up the last segment of the traditional profile of education in Korea. In an effort to help older citizens gain meaningful employment in the rapidly developing industrial-technical sector, the government has established schools, mainly in the larger cities, whose function is to help the older person to find a place in the work force. People attending these adult education centers often are from rural areas and have moved to the city to find economic security.

In summary, Korea places a great emphasis on a centralized education system with periodic local and national examinations. Centralization ensures standardized learning for all students. This does not suggest that intellectual stagnation is fostered; rather, all children are given an equal opportunity to compete and to move into the higher levels of academic life. The homogeneity of Korean society allows certain assumptions to be made about the Korean students; external factors such as language, race, and family are similar throughout the peninsula. Therefore, the competitive examination system, which holds the key to moving up the levels of academe, theoretically is culturally, linguistically, and ethnically fair.

TEACHERS COLLEGES
IN TRANSITION

The history of the Korean people stretches back more than 5,000 years, and although the Korean peninsula has experienced numerous struggles and divisions over the centuries, the Korean people have always managed to reunite as a single, homogeneous nation sharing a common language and culture combining the values of Confucianism, Buddhism, and native religions.

Dr. Moon Yong-lin, 1991

Korea has 13 institutions of higher education that are responsible for the preservice education of all public elementary school teachers. Eleven of these are national teachers colleges that, in 1983, were changed from normal (in the old sense of the American normal schools) or junior colleges to baccalaureate degree-granting institutions. Korea National Education College, an experimental college, also has been authorized to train elementary school teachers. The only non-governmental school that is authorized to prepare public school teachers is the prestigious woman's institution, Ewha University, which is located in suburban Seoul.

Because all preservice elementary teacher education programs are under the strict control of the Ministry of Education, they all offer essentially the same programs of study. Thus generalizations can be made rather broadly. As a result, I will not focus on any one of the 13 programs, but rather on the protocols to be found throughout the system. I had the opportunity to visit seven of the colleges that prepare elementary school teachers. Each has a distinctive campus, method of operation, administration, and professoriate; yet all strictly conform to the policies and guidelines established by the national government and the Ministry of Education. Personnel selection, funding, curriculum, admissions policies, graduation requirements, calendars, events, enrollment patterns, and degree offerings are all under the purview of the Ministry of Education.

The emphasis that the Korean people place on education is a principal reason for the nation's rapid development since 1953. But the desire for a good education is related only partly to the economic and social forces of modern times. Much of the motivation to become educated arises out of the Confucian tradition, which came to ancient Korea from China. In the Confucian ideal one can achieve a position of leadership only through years of scholarship and by passing numerous examinations. Historically, the examinations were based on the Confucian classics. When the system operated fairly and correctly, outstanding scholars emerged into positions of power; nepotism and favoritism were the main casualties of the Confucian education and examination model. The result was excellence in government, education, the arts, sciences, and diplomacy throughout much of Korean history.

In 1910 Japan ruthlessly occupied Korea and immediately attempted to end Korean culture and social life by imposing Japanese will throughout the peninsula. During the occupation, the benefits of education were realized only by those Koreans willing to forgo their culture and civilization. The Korean language, one of the most sophisticated of all languages, was outlawed, as were all other aspects of traditional Korean life. Abuse of Korean women by Japanese soldiers was common, and a total denigration of all things Korean was systematically carried out by the Japanese invaders. The many contributions that Korean civilization made to the historical and cultural development of Japan were distorted or hidden in the historical record.

During the Japanese occupation, only about half of all Korean children were able to attend private schools; few matriculated to high school, and only a very small percentage were admitted to universities in Korea or Japan. The main university in Korea during the Japanese occupation was Keijo (Seoul) Imperial University, which was established mainly for Japanese children living in Korea. A few Koreans who were seen as loyal to the mission of Japanese imperialism were admitted.

School teachers were either Japanese nationals or Koreans who had accepted Japan as their master. The Japanese language was the medium of instruction, and only themes acceptable to the Japanese education authorities were addressed from first grade through college. Students and teachers who deviated from the strict guidelines imposed by the Japanese were suspended, and many were incarcerated and tortured. Women had few opportunities for academic and economic advancement during the Japanese occupation.

Shortly after the end of World War II, teachers colleges were established in each province of southern Korea under the auspices of the United States. However, the Korean War (1951-1953) prevented normal development of formal teacher education on the peninsula. It was not until the Armistice Agreement in the summer of 1953 and the military division of the peninsula at the 38th parallel that teacher education began again on a formal and systematic basis.

Examination Hell

Admission to a college or university in Korea is predicated on passing a highly competitive national entrance examination. Differences in university admission quotas, a large number of applicants, and a substantial group of repeaters (who may not have gotten into their first-choice school) add to the intensity of competition at each examination time. The problem of accommodating students has been exacerbated in recent years by an increase in the number of young people completing the academic high school with little increase in the number of openings at colleges and universities.

In contemporary South Korea a student's success or failure on the college entrance examination is perhaps the single most important factor in determining his or her chances for satisfying employment. Thus a form of "academic Darwinism" can be observed; entrance into a prestigious school becomes the focus of dedication, energy, and self-sacrifice. Often referred to as "examination hell," the national college/university entrance examination, which is required for all students who wish to attend any public or private college, is composed solely of objective, graded tests that are given in the summer after the senior year in high school. A marathon of cramming and tutoring is required for a student to be successful. Many persons I interviewed suggested that the "examination hell" faced by Korean students surpasses similar ordeals in Taiwan, Singapore, China, or even Japan.

During the Yi Dynasty (1392-1910) the examination system was designed to prepare an elite group to move into positions of governmental and societal power and leadership. It was intended to meet two objectives: to bring the best and the brightest into positions of influence and to prevent nepotism and favoritism from being the sole vehicles of upward mobility. This examination system, which had its genesis in dynastic China, was an attempt at democratizing upward mobility in Korea and adding fresh blood to the leadership class. The system worked well through most of the 500 years of the Yi Dynasty; only toward the end of that age did corruption devalue the system. The classical examination, based on the writings and interpretations of Confucius, also became progressively irrelevant as Western scientific ideas began to dominate the nation's modernization.

In modern Korea, the examination system is important not only to those who desire to join the elites in business and society, but also for a substantial portion of the population who wish to hold even modest middle-class positions. Students who fail the examination are

27

faced with dramatically reduced prospects for economic advancement, marrying well, or having any type of opportunity to gain a foothold — even through years of hard work and dedication to employment — in middle- and upper-class society. Parents make their children aware of these harsh realities at an early age and drive their offspring to succeed.

Nevertheless, many of the 2.3 million students who attend junior high schools do not matriculate to the formal high school level. And only about 40% of the students who complete the ninth grade attend academic high schools; a much larger percentage go on to general, vocational, or technical secondary schools. In 1992 approximately 35% of the 1,475,000 students who graduated from an academic high school passed the national entrance examination and began their college education.

Universities in Korea are arranged in a hierarchy according to their prestige and admissions policies. The most prestigious institutions are Seoul National University, Ewha Woman's University, Yonsei University, Korea University, and Sogang University. Under current Ministry of Education policy, prior to sitting for the national examination, a student must declare the institution that he or she plans to attend. If the student's score on the national examination does not meet with the minimum requirements for acceptance to the specific school, the student must wait a full year before retaking the test. As a consequence, many students choose less prestigious universities where they will have a better chance of gaining admission.

Future teachers face the same rigorous path to admission to one of the teachers colleges. For high school students, a typical day begins with study before school and ends with study late into the evening. Weekends and holidays bring little respite. The examination's "facts-only" approach demands rote learning with little room for creative thinking. However, students' creativity does not appear to be impaired in other ways, contrary to the views of some writers. One needs only to visit art museums, attend concerts and plays, or discuss literature, medicine, and other topics with students to recognize that Korean young people are as free-thinking and creative as their counterparts in the West.

Dr. Kwak Dyong-sun suggested: "Of all the students in the world, Koreans spend the largest number of hours studying. There is a saying, '4 pass, 5 fail,' which means that if one sleeps for only four hours a day, he or she may pass the entrance examination; but those who sleep for five hours fail" (Kwak 1991). The stresses an average

18-year-old and his or her family face during this "examination hell," which can extend up to three years, takes its toll. Many Korean young adults will cope with lifelong psychological and physical problems as a result. Furthermore, government examination policies seem to be in a constant a state of flux, which compounds the stress that students must endure.

Prospects for changing this draconian examination system are few. The virtue of the objective testing is its fairness. Although harsh and dispiriting for many, the system is seen by the Korean public as impartial. It allows even the poorest boy or girl who is willing to commit to the rigors of academic life a chance to enter a good college and move to a higher economic and social status.

Admission to a teachers college not only depends on a satisfactory score on the entrance examination, but also on being in good physical and psychological condition. All candidates are required to participate in an interview and take tests of personality and aptitude administered by the college. Regardless of their qualifications, applicants who are crippled, have tuberculosis, or are color-blind are not admitted (Seoul National Teachers College *Bulletin* 1992).

For those who are admitted to teacher education, certain benefits and privileges are part of being accepted at a teachers college. For the future teachers, there is no required tuition; rather, the Ministry of Education subsidizes all freshmen, sophomores, juniors, and seniors. Scholarships also are available to students to help pay for other college-related expenses. These benefits are not given to other university students.

In 1992 about 16,000 students were enrolled in the teachers colleges. The freshman class of 1992 numbered approximately 3,650. A majority of these students came from the lower economic classes; many of them were from rural families that do not have the financial reserves to send their children to college. The tuition-free/scholarship programs ensure that a student from an impoverished background will have an opportunity to improve his or her status through higher education and a teaching career. In turn, the student commits to teach for the same number of years that his or her education was subsidized.

For male students, the four-year degree program is usually interrupted, since Korean males are required to spend 20 months in national military service. Students normally put in their required service between their sophomore and junior years, returning to complete their education at the same college. One college president told me: "Generally this is not a problem; however, many of the boys returning have

29

a different world view and have ideas and values that are not always healthy. They have learned to drink and smoke while in the service and also have been exposed to girls of disrepute."

Korean students frequently say that they feel let down after completing high school and entering the university. The senior year of high school and the examination for university admission are so overwhelmingly important that a sense of melancholy often results upon completion. And the university years seldom are as stimulating as expected. Most Korean college students pass through their four years of higher education with minimal effort. Acceptance at a university is tantamount to graduating. Assignments, lectures, and homework are seen as anticlimactic to the super-charged years of high school. Although deep and lasting friendships are often made at the university, the general mood on the university campus is one of academic lethargy.

Teacher Education Curriculum

At the heart of Korean teacher education is the curriculum. As used in the context of this monograph, I define curriculum as a course of study that, when mastered, gives the prospective teacher a body of knowledge, a sense of values, and a repertoire of teaching techniques. The course comprises classes that are offered so as to form a synergistic, interrelated program.

Two schools of thought dominate the field of curriculum in Korean teacher education. One posits that it is imperative for the student to be steeped in academic subject matter. Courses in mathematics, science, history, language, and the arts and humanities make a strong curriculum; and pedagogical techniques will appear naturally if the student is well-versed in the academic disciplines.

The second, more dominant school of thought posits that the ability to teach a subject is more important than advanced training in a specialized subject area. This second school of thought is led by a group of scholars, most of whom earned their doctoral degrees in education in the United States and were influenced by the utilitarian-instrumental philosophies of William James and John Dewey.

This dichotomy has been current in Korean educational philosophy for many years. As to which will prevail in the training of teachers — academic or pedagogic training — the question remains open to debate. The ideal, of course, is a meld of the two; however, reaching the perfect balance is hampered by the various scholars' subjective values, often based on their own preservice education.

A curriculum is indicative of a number of things: It tells the researcher what the society values in terms of skills and behaviors; it suggests the level of scholarly development of a school or college; and it reflects not only the history of the society, but also how the leadership hopes to shape the society for the future. The importance of curricular organization and development makes it a topic that must be explored in order to understand modern Korean teacher education.

The curriculum of the national teachers colleges places a good deal of emphasis on subjects related to Korean identity and pride. From 25% to 30% of the classes fit this definition. Programs of study in the academic high schools and at other colleges and universities also place a significant emphasis on "Koreanism." The reason for this focus is the desire of the leadership to establish a national identity that separates Korea from its long history of Chinese influence and Japanese captivity. Only since 1953 has South Korea seen itself as an independent entity; even now tensions persist between Seoul and P'yŏngyang, the capital of North Korea. Much of South Korea's independence also is tied to America and its role as Korea's military and trade ally. My interviews in Korea suggest that an agenda of this curricular focus is to diminish feelings of cultural inferiority that have resulted from Korea's history of foreign occupation and domination.

Korean culture is splendid in itself. An intact Korean civilization can be traced back to the 7th century, when the Three Kingdoms of ancient times were united, making this peninsular nation the second oldest intact society on earth after China. Only through education can the Korean culture be perpetuated. Korea's education leaders strongly believe that new generations will be able to retain their cultural identity only if their teachers themselves are aware of their cultural legacies.

The teachers colleges' basic goal is to train quality school teachers for the elementary schools of Korea. All elementary teacher training is done in government colleges, with the exception of Ewha University, which is private. Students' expenses are government-subsidized, and the enrollees are very bright and competitive. Upon graduation, all are guaranteed jobs in elementary education. Students usually are required to live in college dormitories, to take their meals together, and to become part of a learning community. The colleges try to instill in these students the view that teaching is a service to the nation and to humankind.

Based on numerous interviews with leading educators, I found that the Korean teacher education leadership bases the college curriculum on the following objectives, which are designed to effect this noble mission:

- To develop a teacher who is mentally and physically well-balanced;
- To cultivate positive character traits and a sense of ethics and morality;
- To enhance national pride in Korean history, culture, and civilization;
- To give breadth to the student's basic knowledge and to allow the student to master skills related to his or her future teaching duties;
- To engender an understanding of and empathy for children;
- To develop professionalism and dedication to teaching as a career;
- To cultivate the desire for lifelong learning;
- To encourage students to pursue higher research in their areas of responsibility and interest; and
- To stimulate eagerness to participate as a leader in the community and in the nation.

Those who develop, modify, and revise the curriculum seek to ensure that the sequence and juxtaposition of learning experiences at the teachers colleges meet the challenges of these nine objectives.

A close friend and colleague, Dr. P.A. Herbert, who is currently a professor at Osaka University and has done extensive research on Japanese culture and education, suggests that "there is in the education systems of all advanced civilizations a dichotomy in aims and methods which reflects two conflicting demands found in all developed societies." Professor Herbert suggests that "all social systems demand a certain degree of order and conformity for the maintenance of civility and law." Conversely, if a society is to advance, it is also necessary to foster originality in technology and cultural matters. This latter requirement often goes hand-in-hand with iconoclastic views and nonconformist actions. Depending on world conditions and the nation's development in economic and social terms, curriculum models may stress either conformity or originality. Balancing the two can appear to be quixotic. Thus teacher education faces a dilemma. To suggest that either emphasis is the sign of a higher level of educational vigor would be a sophistry. Extremes in curriculum design in either direction will produce undesirable results for the nation.

The curriculum in the teachers colleges in Korea is similar for all students who select elementary education as their future career. The curriculum assumes that elementary teachers need a combination of interrelated, mutually supportive learning experiences. The curriculum requires the preservice teacher to complete 180 credits during a four-year period. (Other baccalaureate programs in Korea are usually 140 credits.) Three components of the curriculum are: 1) general education, 2) a major field of study, and 3) pedagogical training and practice.

General education, I discovered from my discussions with leading Korean educators, is intended to cultivate broad, basic knowledge and to expand the student's vision of society, knowledge of Korean history and ethics, language skills, and humanistic orientation. The goal is to eliminate narrow thinking and create a truly educated person.

This concept of general education can be traced to two historical periods: the Golden Age of Greece and the Age of Confucius in China. During Greece's Golden Age an educated person was capable of dealing with numerous topics, ranging from politics to poetry; this tradition was revived during the European Renaissance and survives in the liberal arts tradition of modern universities in the West. An equally important parallel developed in Asia. Confucius began a multi-arts tradition that has lasted in much of the Orient into the contemporary era. Koreans also believe that education for moral and ethical character, a Confucian ideal, is congruent with the goals of general education.

In the Korean teachers colleges, general education classes are a major part of the four-year curriculum. The content of general education comprises work in ethics, the humanities, social sciences, Korean and foreign languages, and mathematical and natural sciences. Korean teachers learn to communicate effectively, in both verbal and written forms; and they develop refined tastes in literature, music, and the performing and visual arts. Understanding the dynamics of politics, economics, and modern history is also an imperative in the curriculum. Other classes in the general education course of study include: computer science, Chinese characters, logic, psychology, sociology, anthropology, law, geography, and family life education. Students complete about 55 credits; some of the classes are required of all teachers college students, and others are electives (Seoul National Teachers College *Bulletin* 1992).

The major field is the next most extensive requirement. A major requires 32 credits taken over the final three years in the baccalaureate degree program, the first year being devoted exclusively to general studies. All elementary education students must declare a major from the various available options. Unlike American teachers colleges, where the major for future elementary teachers invariably is "elementary education," the colleges in Korea want their students to study in depth a specific field or discipline that is related to elementary education.

Prior to the advent of the first teachers college movement in Korea (1946-1953), all education tended to be in the liberal arts. Influenced mainly by the United States, Korea began programs during the post-Korean War decade that added to students' understanding of social sciences and technology. After the transformation of the Korean teachers colleges from two-year colleges to four-year, degree-granting institutions in 1981-1983, authorities placed even greater emphasis on specialization as part of the new curriculum. The training of specialists is now part of the mandate of the four-year teachers colleges.

A review of the literature on pre-1981 teacher education suggests that general education and pedagogic studies dominated the curriculum. Educational authorities in Seoul then realized that elementary teachers needed to be trained in one or two specialized areas in order for them to develop the in-depth knowledge and research abilities necessary to deal with increasing specialization in all fields of endeavor. This concept is particularly true in the various disciplines of science, which change rapidly. Thus the teachers colleges in modern Korea now require their students to declare a field of "subject matter specialization." These majors are administered at the departmental level; and the college teachers are specialists themselves with advanced academic degrees, usually at minimum a master's degree from a Korean university.

Typically, the following majors are available: Korean language education, ethics education, social studies education, mathematics education, science education, physical education, music education, fine arts education, practical/vocational arts education, foreign language education, and elementary education. Each of these disciplines is mutually exclusive, though students majoring in one field may choose electives from another. Though all who graduate from the Korean teachers colleges receive elementary teacher certification, each teacher may be assigned special duties at his or her school related to the major area.

The third component of teacher preparation concentrates on pedagogical classes and field work. Emphasis is on teaching methodology, child development, educational psychology, research and statistics, classroom management, and educational history, philosophy, and sociology. Future teachers do their practice teaching in college-affiliated elementary schools located on the same campus as the college. I visited a number of these outstanding elementary schools, which are administered by a principal under the authority of the college president, and found excellent teachers. A preservice teacher will practice under the watchful eye of a master elementary teacher. The synergistic relationship between the teachers college and the affiliated laboratory school is mutually beneficial and enhances the practical aspect of the teaching/learning process.

In summary, all elementary school teachers are both generalists and specialists, which in Korea's expanding and competitive elementary education system is both practical and efficient.

Teachers College Faculty

Currently in Korea there are some 556 two-year colleges, four-year colleges, and universities, employing approximately 42,000 faculty members for about 1.5 million students. These figures represent a significant increase over the immediate post-World War II picture. In 1945, when Korea was liberated from the Japanese occupation, there were only 19 higher education institutions with a faculty of 1,930 and 7,819 students.

An equally positive expansion has occurred in the teachers colleges, which now have more than 700 faculty members serving some 16,000 students. The retention rate for professors exceeds 95%, reflecting a high level of satisfaction. My interviews suggest that frustrations do exist, but in general faculty members are mostly satisfied with their career and the college in which they teach. I found that older faculty members usually expressed a greater degree of contentment than younger faculty members, but the variation between old and young was minor.

Faculty profiles at the teachers colleges in Korea are changing, as the Ministry of Education attempts to enhance this important component of the nation's education program. Although each teachers college faculty profile is slightly different from the others, about a quarter of the faculty hold Ph.D. degrees and another 30% are A.B.D. (all but dissertation). Most of the remainder have one or more master's degrees and are encouraged to pursue a doctorate.

When the teachers colleges were upgraded from junior- to senior-level institutions between 1981 and 1983, faculty who were employed during the junior-college phase (circa 1946-1983) were retained under a tenure policy that exists at all national colleges and universities. As these faculty members, many of whom hold only a master's degree, retire, the Ministry of Education has indicated its determination to fill the resulting vacancies with Ph.D. (or A.B.D.) holders. I should note here that very few faculty members at the teachers colleges hold a Ph.D. earned outside Korea. Seoul National University and the other distinguished colleges and universities, such as Ewha Woman's University, employ relatively large percentages of professors with doctorates from American, Japanese, or European universities.

Faculty rank and promotion are based on a predetermined number of years of service, excellence in teaching and writing, advanced degrees, and publications of major research findings. The ranks begin with lecturer and progress to instructor (usually for three years), assistant professor (four years), associate professor (five years), and finally to professor. All appointments and promotions are made by the Ministry of Education, as are all dismissals. College presidents are appointed by the Ministry of Education after being elected to that position by the faculty.

Faculty at the teachers colleges are employed on the basis of two general criteria: 1) the needs of the college and 2) the credentials of the candidate. Each college is responsible for ensuring that all positions are properly staffed. When a position becomes available, the college and the Ministry of Education advertise the vacancy. The new faculty member must first be approved by the college faculty and administration; then he or she is either approved or rejected by the Ministry of Education in Seoul. Because first employment is tantamount to lifetime employment, great care is taken to select the best candidate. New college teachers do not need to have been public school teachers, although many I interviewed had begun their careers in public education.

All new college teachers are encouraged to continue their education, and generous grants and release time are made available so that they may complete their doctorates. The major goals of faculty development are to increase the number of professors with the Ph.D. degree and to re-orient the faculty away from purely teaching duties to teaching and action-oriented research activities.

An interesting gender contradiction exists among faculty and students: Virtually all faculty members are male, while most of the students being admitted to elementary education are female.

According to Dr. Chang In-suk, Secretary-General of the prestigious Korean Council for University Education, "Some 75% of teachers college enrollments are women students. This is an indication that elementary teaching is more attractive to female students than male students" (1988). At one school, Cheju National Teachers College located on the island of Cheju, all of the freshmen students admitted in 1992 were women. However, the president of that college told me that new admissions policies should bring about a greater degree of gender balance in the student population.

Authorities who oversee teachers college admissions at the Ministry of Education indicate that the ideal is a 50-50 balance of men and women in teacher training. Whether this goal can be achieved without distorting the objective criteria for college admission presents an interesting issue for Korea. The main attractions that a teachers college education affords women are: 1) job security, 2) financial aid to attend college, 3) stable employment, 4) geographical mobility that can complement their husband's career, 5) excellent benefits (in spite of relatively low salaries), 6) time off to have and raise children with a liberal job-return policy, 7) work hours compatible with their children's school day, and 8) relatively high status in what is otherwise a male-dominated society. Disincentives for males to become elementary school teachers are low wages and little opportunity to advance rapidly despite hard work, excellent skills, and intelligence.

College Facilities

Facilities are similar among the teachers colleges. For example, national law requires, "as for school land area, this should be more than five times the total area taken by school buildings. . . ." Furthermore, "as for library facilities, an institution should be equipped with a periodical room, stack room, an administrative room, in addition to a reading room with a minimum of seating capacity of 10% of the total number of students" (Chang 1988).

Professors and administrators are provided with good office space. Tea and coffee are available in the various teachers' lounges, and food service is excellent and inexpensive. I was impressed with the cleanliness and orderliness of the campuses I visited. Walls are free of unsightly graffiti, although announcement posters abound. Students can be found reading or talking as they lounge on the spacious lawns that characterize Korean colleges and universities. I found the general atmosphere of the campuses upbeat and exciting.

Teachers colleges are well-funded. The Ministry of Education maintains a budget specific to the ongoing personnel, student, facility, and expansion needs of the teachers colleges. Although the actual budget is undifferentiated in the overall national education budget, making it difficult to examine specifics, I learned from colleagues in the Ministry of Education that the per-student allocation for prospective teachers is the highest among the undergraduate programs in Korea.

Problems Facing Teacher Education

Perhaps the most difficult issue that faces administrators and faculty is the removal of a professor. No dismissal mechanism exists unless the person has broken legal or moral codes. Poor teaching skills, lack of research, or failure to continue education will not result in the removal of a faculty member once he or she has been promoted to the rank of assistant professor. To quote one college president, "I really have no way to dismiss or punish a member of my faculty, even if he is incompetent, unless he does something terrible with the students or gets in trouble with the authorities."

A general problem facing teacher education is the "top-down" organizational framework under which the teachers colleges function. Control, in terms of funding and major decision making with regard to all aspects of the educational program, is vested in the highest levels of government. Mandates filter down from the Ministry of Education to the individual institutions.

Clearly, the governance of colleges and universities by a central Ministry of Education is quite different from American higher education governance at the national level. Yet on close inspection, the system used *within* various U.S. states for public higher education governance is similar to the top-down Korean model. Central authority often rests in the hands of a Board of Higher Education appointed by a governor. Operational aspects of the system are delegated to a chancellor or commissioner, who oversees various bureaucracies that are responsible for finance, law, lobbying, administration, personnel, and so on. Presidents of the state's junior colleges, four-year colleges, and universities report to the chancellor or commissioner, who in turn is responsible to the governor's office and the governing board. Although the American system prides itself on "decentralization," state higher education governance frequently is as centralized as that found at the national level in South Korea. The main difference, of course, is that the United States Department of Education, the closest American equivalent to Korea's Ministry of Education, does not have the same degree of control over the educative process.

38

One advantage of a nationally centralized administration is that the Ministry of Education is able to anticipate and respond to teacher placement needs rapidly. Should a shortage of elementary educators be projected, the entrance examination system can be adapted to channel more students into the field. The reverse is also true.

Korea's Future Elementary Teachers

Completion of the degree requirements at any of the 11 national teachers colleges, Ewha Woman's University, or the new Korea National Education University leads directly to certification as a teacher for grades one to six. Licensure in Korea is national, not under the auspices of the provincial governments. Most teachers return to their native provinces to teach, and many single graduates return to live with their parents until they marry. Others attempt to gain employment in Seoul, Korea's most appealing city, which currently has a population in excess of 10 million (probably nearer 14 million including the new satellite cities that are quickly filling the Han River Valley).

Continuing education opportunities abound for new teachers, especially if they teach in cities like Pusan and Seoul. In 1991, nearly 50,000 teachers took part in continuing education workshops. Inservice requirements and the desire to work toward a master's degree while fully employed move both new and veteran teachers to seek out opportunities for continued learning. Added education also can affect a teacher's salary. Salary increases are based on a complex formula designed by the Department of Teacher Education at the Ministry of Education. The formula takes into account years of service and additional education.

Requests for transfers also are approved or denied by the Ministry of Education. Detailed records are kept at the ministry on all teachers. Generally, this central system is regarded as fair; the teachers I interviewed expressed few concerns, except for believing that their salaries are too low. Although teachers in Korea, especially university professors, tend to enjoy higher status than their Western counterparts, they often say that they are overworked and underpaid. Large gifts of money given to teachers by students' parents are not uncommon in Korea but are officially illegal.

In the spring of 1989, an independent union was formed for the benefit of the nation's teachers. The aims of the National Teachers Union include improving salaries and working conditions for all teachers and reforming the Ministry of Education, which some educators believe is too influential and politicized. However, official labor union status was not granted to the National Teachers Union, because Korean teachers are considered to be civil servants and thus, under current law, do not have the right to strike.

Many older educators believe that unionism will erode the high status given to educators. This is a common view in academic circles. However, the *Asian Wall Street Journal* (5 December 1989) reported that the union had the support of 82% of all teachers. Problems arising from disputes between pro-union teachers and the Ministry of Education surface regularly, and tension continues to exist over the issue of unionization itself. Many of the parents of prospective teachers that I met were made uneasy by this new problem. Unlike Japan, where teachers unions are both powerful and disruptive, Korea has no tradition of unionism for public school teachers. How powerful the teachers union may become and what the reaction of the national government will be remains to be seen.

Meanwhile, at the official level, an effort currently is under way to reduce class sizes in the public elementary schools. The reduction will be accomplished by admitting more students to the field of elementary education and increasing incentives to become public school teachers, such as raising salaries and improving working conditions.

A CRITICAL ANALYSIS
OF KOREAN
TEACHER EDUCATION

Coming close to the threshold of the 21st century we see new challenges looming largely as a result of continual industrialization and growing inter-dependency among nations.

Dr. Hong Woong-sun, *Koreana*, 1991

Because of its importance, complexity, and historical evolution, elementary teacher education plays a major part in the education system of South Korea. Scholars, both inside and outside of academe, have expressed views on how teacher education can be improved and how existing paradigms can be transformed. It is vitally important to any organization that critics be encouraged to express legitimate concerns and to offer solutions. However, when a foreign researcher visits another society, it is important to temper critical analysis with sensitivity. Thus, the following criticism of Korea's teachers colleges is derived not only from my own limited experience, but also from critical literature on Korean teacher education. Much of this literature is written by distinguished Korean educators who, from firsthand knowledge, years of experience, and deep and sincere concern, are disturbed by the training of teachers in their society.

Anticipating the Need for New Teachers

One of the major issues that confronts Korea's education leaders is anticipating the number of elementary teachers that will be needed in the future. Too few teachers will mean increases in class size; too many will cause problems in teacher placement, increase schools' financial problems, and perhaps result in unemployment for teachers. Ideally, the number of teachers produced by the teachers colleges should allow a general reduction of the student-teacher ratio but not limit job opportunities for teachers in terms of their choice of school location or subject of specialization.

Over the years a severe shortage of teachers has developed in certain fields of expertise. Mathematics, computer studies, and the natural sciences are fields in which there is a paucity of candidates. A solution now being explored is to allow graduates of regular liberal arts and science colleges to take a one- or two-year postgraduate program at a teachers college to obtain conditional teacher certification.

This would help to solve the immediate problem, but it could encourage students to avoid teacher education initially and enter the profession only when the non-education job market became hostile to them. Some Korean critics feel that this solution would not engender a commitment to education on the part of students who see teaching as a "fail-safe" occupation.

The transformation in the early 1980s of the teachers colleges from two-year to four-year institutions, which increased the requirements for becoming a teacher, has not resulted in a significant increase in teachers' salaries. And Korea's supercharged economy makes employment outside of the field of education desirable, especially for those, like new would-be teachers, with a baccalaureate degree.

A related problem is low prestige. Elementary school teaching commands a lower status than secondary school or college teaching. Evidence suggests that, whenever possible, elementary teachers try to move into junior high school teaching positions through inservice experiences; but movement in the opposite direction seldom is seen. Though the concept of inservice education is part of the Korean tradition, it also has led to some problems. Upon completion of a fixed number of college-level specialization courses, an elementary teacher may seek employment in a junior high school. Thus, too often, skilled and highly motivated teachers leave the elementary setting to become part of the secondary school system.

The major transformation of the college system has helped to resolve this problem. To enter the four-year teachers college, elementary education students must first complete the academic high school. This requirement gives them more time and greater experience to decide if they wish to spend their careers as elementary teachers. However, one critic suggested that, while "the quality of students has been increased; the quality of the professoriate has not kept pace."

Problems in Academe

Inside academe, the gulf between academics and pedagogy continues to be a taxing problem. A review of the teachers college catalogues suggests that no way has yet been found to bridge this gulf to everyone's satisfaction. It is to be hoped that constant adjustments to the balance of courses, use of a common institutional environment, and encouragement to professors in both areas to be co-supportive will enable students to master both the esoteric and the pragmatic elements of teaching. Assessing the success of this synthesis seems to be impossible; in exploring the literature on the subject and speaking

44

with academicians in Korea and the United States, I was unable to find valid assessment models. Students do integrate subject matter and methodology; they do become good teachers. So, perhaps, formal assessment is less essential than lively debate, which keeps students and their professors focused on the need to balance knowledge and technique.

A second problem inside academe arises from the teaching methodology of most professors of education, who are seen as too often relying on the lecture method. Although this style conveys information, teachers, students, and educational psychologists believe that students should spend more instructional time in group discussions and seminars. As a lecturer at a number of colleges and universities in Korea, I noticed that obviously bright and interested students tended to internalize their feelings and seldom were responsive during question-and-answer periods. Skill in discussion can be obtained only through practice, in which Korean students have been limited by the instructional methods their professors use.

Working Toward Gender Balance

Korean educators also are trying to address the issue of a disproportionate number of women in teaching. The ratio of women to men continues to grow. Some educators suggest that this trend will be deleterious to the sociology of the educative process and that a better balance of the sexes is desirable. To set up quotas for the number of men and women admitted to teachers colleges would deny equal opportunity. However, to some extent, teachers colleges have attempted to achieve greater balance by manipulating the scores on the national entrance examination. In doing so, the Ministry of Education not only can select highly qualified students, but also can arrange a proportionate number of men and women to be admitted to the training.

Men who do attend the teachers colleges tend to go into the fields of mathematics, science, and the social studies; while women gravitate to the languages, elementary education, and the performing arts. Thus, the root of the shortages in male-oriented specializations is the low number of males who enter elementary education.

The explanation for the gender imbalance is tied to economics. Women in Korea are more concerned with a job that provides the hours, benefits, security, and vacation time that is compatible with their lifestyles; men are more concerned with a high salary and rapid upward mobility, which they cannot attain in a teaching career.

45

Teaching at the elementary level offers the kinds of rewards most women seek. As a consequence, after five years of "pay-back service," many men leave teaching for more lucrative positions in business, law, or government service.

Status and Sociological Issues

Teacher status, mentioned previously, also is the focus of another sort of problem. Research by Korean scholars, which I was able to confirm in my interviews, suggests that a measure of "status anxiety" ripples through the education profession. In traditional Korean society, teachers are held in high regard. However, their relatively low salaries in comparison to other professions make teachers less satisfied with their career choice. Thus teachers themselves tend to devalue the public's esteem for the teaching profession. These contradictions create status anxieties for both education students and the established teachers.

Korean educators have identified five critical factors for the person selecting a career in elementary education. The future teacher must have a certain idealism about teaching and love the life of scholarship. He or she also must enjoy being with children and find teaching children fulfilling. The future teacher must want: 1) high prestige, which is particularly the case for teachers in the smaller towns; 2) job security; and 3) economic security. (Although salaries are not high, teachers receive numerous health and retirement benefits, and they are not required to pay taxes on their income.)

A sociological issue, which may become a problem in the future, is that teachers generally come from lower-middle-class backgrounds and rural families. A disproportionate number are from farm families or from fishing backgrounds. Such a background often engenders an orientation toward authority, order, and discipline. Yet Korea is changing rapidly, becoming a modern, technological-industrial society that depends increasingly on independent and creative thinking. Thus the blind allegiance to authority that once characterized most Asian societies now is regarded as a less positive characteristic.

Governance Reforms

The national entrance examination, which previously was discussed in some detail, presents certain problems for the elementary teacher training system. Taken after 12th grade, this very difficult competitive test (in 1992, only 35% of the candidates passed) is used to channel students into the teachers colleges. Competition for admission to higher education programs is so strong that great stress is placed on the students. Korean leaders have begun to question whether the examination system is the best way to select future teachers, and so they currently are reviewing other schemes for selection and admission into the baccalaureate teachers colleges.

Reforms also are being considered within the Ministry of Education. National law gives the ministry control or significant influence over all aspects of education policy; it is particularly powerful when dealing with issues related to "national" colleges and universities, which include the teachers colleges. Unlike the United States, where universities have considerable autonomy in developing their faculties and curricula, teachers colleges in Korea are required to adhere to policy guidelines set forth by the Ministry of Education. In fairness to this governmental department, it must be said that the Ministry's concern for quality, equity, and the expansion of educational opportunities is impressive. But, as with most bureaucracies, the ministry is slow to resolve policy matters; and decisions are perhaps too influenced by the political concerns of the central government.

The Ministry of Education has not been able to solve those naturally arising tensions that exist in most developed countries between central authority and local autonomy, as represented by college presidents. Korean college presidents, who serve for four years, bring continuity to the administration and decision-making process. Their appointments usually are based on academic credentials, excellence in research and teaching, success in previous administrative positions, and perceived potential as leaders of campus life. All have advanced degrees and are elected by the faculty and then confirmed by the ministry.

The last, perhaps most significant issue to confront elementary teacher education is related to fundamental pedagogical philosophy. Are teachers born or can they be trained? Can tests be used to determine who has the potential to be an effective teacher? Is the best education for a teacher to be found in a specialized area of expertise, such as mathematics or Korean literature, or is it the "science of education" with its focus on methodology and curriculum?

Ultimately, the question is, Are teachers colleges necessary? This concern is being actively addressed by professors, administrators, and Ministry of Education officials in Korea.

A significant group of scholars, basically from liberal arts and sciences colleges, believe that departments of elementary and secondary education should be incorporated into the major universities and that teachers colleges should be converted into regular, comprehensive institutions or become branch campuses of existing comprehensive universities. These advocates of integrating teacher education into the general university contend that more than two-thirds of the coursework future teachers take consists of general studies and academic classes; only one-third is directly related to pedagogy. These scholars believe that the cross-fertilization of knowledge between students of the arts and sciences and of the pedagogical studies would be beneficial to faculty and students and would improve the climate of the institutions.

Most professors of teacher education with whom I spoke take exception to this notion. They believe that teacher training should not be subsumed by the regular universities. Teaching is not only a profession, these scholars contend, it is a mission; and specialized training in an isolated, focused environment is the best way to create the knowledge base and the commitment needed to become an elementary school teacher.

Those who advocate the integrated approach refer to the American experience as their model. Those who maintain the more traditional view favor the French paradigm, which suggests that teachers are part of the national defense of the nation and should be given special training, benefits, and privileges.

Underwood's Views

Horace G. Underwood, whose grandfather was one of the pioneer American Christian missionaries in Korea (circa 1885), has spent his life as an advocate for Korean culture and independence. Born in Korea in 1917 and heir to the Underwood Typewriter Company, Underwood was a professor and also president of Yansei University in Seoul. He has been a long-time observer of Korean society. Underwood's observations about modern Korean education, though general in nature, are applicable to the teachers college model.

Underwood contends that, since the liberation from Japan, when the education system was a "basket case," Korean education has made great strides and has become very successful. Koreans exhibit "zeal for education" that "is reflected in all aspects of Korean school life. There has never been a need for truant officers in Korea. Here everybody wants to go to school," says Underwood. The result is that Korea is perhaps the most literate nation on earth. The schools experience few discipline problems, and the populace are eager to improve themselves and their progeny through the educative process. Yet modern Korea also must deal with numerous interconnected educational problems, all of which will be difficult to resolve. Underwood states:

> The irony is, the very thing that has made Korea strong is perhaps a kind of weakness. Under the premodern Confucian educational system, social advancement was through memorizing the Confucian classics in order to pass a rote examination. The successful candidates in the fiercely competitive state examination promptly rated appointment to a sensitive government post and *yangban* or "noble" status.
>
> Thus the Korean people's eagerness for education is in many ways an eagerness for status rather than content, for certification rather than for an education, for membership in an elite department of an elite university rather than following a particular field of study. To counter the evil effects of this struggle for elite status and to meet a widespread demand for a more egalitarian society, the government has taken various steps to 'equalize' education. Even so, starting at the kindergarten level, parents try to enter their children in "prestigious" schools in order that they may eventually have a better chance to enter a prestigious university.
>
> This tendency is most clearly visible at the time of applying to enter university, when choices of school and departments are made at the last minute, on the basis of the competition ratios, rather than on the student's occupational goals. (Underwood 1991, pp. 63-64)

Underwood believes that this type of decision making adversely influences education at the university, because many students apply to departments in which they have no real interest, simply in the hope of obtaining admission. Once accepted, they pursue programs, usually to completion, but without real purpose.

Another problem, according to Underwood, is the quota system for assigning students to various academic departments. Says Underwood, "Schools are not allowed to open new 'departments' without government permission and the opening of a new department always means the enrollment of a quota of students in that field." Underwood continues:

> The quota system of itself may not be all bad. . . . But in practice it leads to several problems, especially at the university level. As applied in Korea today, the student may apply to only one department of one university each year. This turns university admission into a kind of academic gamble as the can-

didate tries to guess which department of which university is the best bet for admission, with personal preference usually taking second place in the choice.

Actual admission is based on a strict "cut-line" score, counting down the requisite quota number of places from the top. One unfortunate result is that many capable candidates who guess wrong fail to enter while less capable students who guessed better get in. (Underwood 1991, pp. 64-65)

As the traditional ascriptive social structure lost its currency through a series of drastic social changes in the late 19th century, education became one of the most powerful means of social and economic mobility for individuals. Changing the education paradigm to address the issues of the rigid tradition, whether in teaching methodology or the examination system, is a challenging goal. The Korean people are fearful that overhauling the system may allow favoritism to creep in, to become a criterion for high school and particularly for university admissions. Now, although draconian in nature, the system is considered fair, even by the harshest of its critics. Balancing innovative education design, particularly in the examination-oriented environment that drives Korean education, with Western notions of the liberal arts and an open education presents a perplexing dilemma for Korean educators.

AFTERWORD

This essay is the result of my continuing interest in comparative education and in Asian education and Korea in particular. My goal in developing this work is to increase communication between two quite disparate societies that, because of geography, historical evolution, ethnological patterns, religious diversities, and philosophical orientation, have developed differently. The United States and Korea not only are on opposite sides of the planet, they represent quite different approaches to issues common to all civilizations — family life, child rearing, value orientations, health and recreation, and pedagogic and educative models.

As I was departing from Korea, the harsh winter season was just beginning. A poem of one of Korea's finest and earliest poets came to mind:

> Autumn winds are blowing:
> I chant a sad song.
> So few people in this world
> have even understood.
> It is the third watch:
> rain splatters the windows.
> I sit in front of the lamp,
> my spirit 10,000 li away.
>
> Ch'oe Chi-won,
> circa 880 A.D.

I am comfortable in saying that the academic goals I set for myself in the project have been met; and my personal knowledge of comparative education, and specifically elementary teachers college education on the Korean peninsula, have been greatly enhanced. I hope that the information presented in this work opens doors of understanding for other scholars.

RESOURCES

The following books, articles, and other documents were useful in my study of Korean education and may prove to be valuable to other researchers. As an introduction to Korean education, I particularly recommend *Koreana: A Quarterly on Korean Culture*, Vol. 5, no. 2, 1991. This English-language journal devoted this issue to education in Korea and includes 14 essays on traditional and contemporary Korean education. In addition, the *Asian Wall Street Journal* and the *Far East Economic Review* are important resources for contemporary comments on Korean education.

Allen, Horace. *Things Korean*. New York: Fleming H. Revell, 1908.

Bae Chong-keun. "Education Top Reason Behind Rapid Growth." *Koreana* 5, no. 2 (1991): 56-63.

Bae Chong-keun, et al. *National Survey on Education*. Seoul: Jing Min, 1988.

Bae Chong-keun and Lee Mee-na. *The Reality of Korean Education*. Seoul: Jing Min, 1988.

Brandt, Vincent S.R. *A Korean Village: Between Farm and Sea*. Cambridge, Mass.: Harvard University Press, 1971.

Chang In-suk, ed. *Korean Higher Education: Its Development, Aspects and Prospects*. Seoul: Korean Council for University Education, 1988.

Charters, A.N., ed. *Comparing Adult Education World Wide*. San Francisco: Jossey-Bass, 1981.

Dix, Griffin. *Studies of Korea in Transition*. Honolulu: University of Hawaii Press, 1979.

Durant, Will. *Our Oriental Heritage*. New York: Simon and Schuster, 1935.

Ewha Woman's University. *Catalogue, 1992*. Seoul, 1992.

Fisher, James E. *Democracy and Mission Education in Korea*. New York: Teachers College of Columbia University Press, 1928.

Gale, James S. *Korea Sketches*. New York: Fleming H. Revell, 1988.

Hall, Sherwood. *With Stethoscope in Asia: Korea*. McLean, Va.: MCL Associates, 1978.

Hoefer, Hans J. *Republic of Korea*. Singapore: APA Publications, 1988.

Hong Say-myung. *Study in Korea*. Seoul: Korea Research Foundation, 1989.

Hong Sung-jik. *A Study of the Korean Values*. Seoul: Korea University Press, 1969.

Hong Sung-jik. "A Study of the Values of College Students." *Journal of Asiatic Studies* 26 (1970): 27-37.

Hong Woong-sun. "Education Experts Offer Lofty Goals." *Koreana* 5, no. 2 (1991): 89-99.

Hyde, Georgie D.M. *South Korea: Education, Culture and Economy*. New York: Macmillan, 1988.

Ignas, Edward, et al. *Comparative Educational Systems*. Itasca, Ill.: F.E. Peacock, 1981.

Jayasuruja, J.E. *Education in Korea: A Third World Success Story*. Seoul: Korea National Commission of UNESCO, 1984.

Joe, Wanne J. *Traditional Korea: A Cultural History*. Seoul: Chungang University Press, 1972.

Kidd, J.R. "Comparing Adult Education Worldwide." In *Comparing Adult Education World Wide*, edited by A.N. Charters. San Francisco: Jossey-Bass, 1981.

Kim Chong-chol. *Education and Development*. Seoul: National University Press, 1985.

Kim, Eugene C. "Education in Korea Under Japanese Colonial Rule." In *Korea Under Japanese Colonial Rule*. Kalamazoo: Western Michigan University Press, 1973.

Kim Jae-un. *The Psychology of the Korean Family*. Seoul: Ewha University Press, 1975.

Kim Jae-un and Kim Kyong-dong. *The Koreans: Their Mind and Behavior*. Seoul: Kyobo Books, 1991.

Kim Kyong-dong. "Social Change and Development in Korea Since 1945: Modernization and Uneven Development." *Korean and World Affairs* 9, no. 4 (1985): 756-88.

Kim Youn-tai. "Business Demands Higher Skilled Grads." *Koreana* 5, no. 2 (1991): 69-80.

Kim Yung-chung, ed. *Women of Korea*. Seoul: Ewha University Press, 1976.

Korean Council for University Education. *Current Issues in University Education*. Seoul, 1987.

Korean Council for University Education. *A Study on Higher Education in Korea, 1986*. Seoul, 1987.

Korea Overseas Information Service. *Korea*. Seoul: KOIS and Samhwa Press, 1990.

Kluckhohn, Clyde. *Mirror for Men*. New York: McGraw-Hill, 1949.

Kluckhohn, C., and Hurray, H.A. *Personality in Nature, Society, and Culture*. New York: Alfred A. Knopf, 1956.

Kwak Dyong-sun. " 'Examination Hell' in Korea Revisited." *Koreana* 5, no. 2 (1991): 45-65.

Ledyand, Gani. *The Dutch Come to Korea and the Journal of Hendrik Homel, 1653-1668*. Seoul: Royal Asiatic Society, Korea Branch, 1971.

Lee Ki-baik. *A New History of Korea*. Seoul, 1984.

Lee Sang-ki. "The Contributions of Education to Economic Growth in Korea, 1975-88." Doctoral dissertation, Dongguk University, Seoul, 1989.

Lee Won-ho. "Modern System Came Hard Way to Korea." *Koreana* 5, no. 2 (1991): 23-30.

Lerner, David. *The Passing of Traditional Society*. New York: Free Press, 1958.

Levine, R.A. *Culture, Behavior and Personality*. Chicago: Aldine, 1973.

Linton, R. *The Cultural Background of Personality*. New York: Appleton-Century, 1945.

Macdonald, Donald Stone. *The Koreans: Contemporary Politics and Society*. Boulder, Colo.: Westview Press, 1990.

Manguno, Joseph D. "Korea Faces Prolonged Clash in Education." *Asian Wall Street Journal*, 5 December 1989, p. 1.

Mason, Edward S., et al. *The Economic and Social Modernization of the Republic of Korea*. Cambridge, Mass: Harvard University Press, 1980.

McGuinn, Noel F., et al. *Education and Development in Korea*. Cambridge, Mass: Harvard University Press, 1980.

Ministry of Education. *Education in Korea, 1990-92*. Pamphlet. Seoul, 1992.

Moon Yong-lin. "Facts About Education Present No Shangri-La." *Koreana* 5, no. 2 (1991): 30-45.

Mortimer, Louis R.; Shaw, William; and Savada, A.M., eds. *South Korea: A Country Study*. Library of Congress Area Handbook Series. Washington, D.C.: Library of Congress, 1992.

Myers, R.H., and Peattie, M.R., eds. *Japanese Colonial Empire, 1895-1945*. Princeton, N.J.: Princeton University Press, 1984.

Nahn, Andrew C. *Korea: Tradition and Transformation: A History of the Korean People*. Hollym Press, 1988.

National Cheju Teachers College. *Bulletin, 1992*. Cheju-do, 1992.

National Inchon Teachers College. *Bulletin, 1990*. Inchon, 1990.

National Pusan Teachers College. *Bulletin, 1990-1992*. Pusan, 1990.

Opter, David. *The Politics of Modernization*. Chicago: University of Chicago Press, 1965.

Osgood, Charles. *The Koreans and Their Culture*. New York: Ronald Press, 1951.

Pak Cun-hui. *Korean Views of Education*. Seoul: Kyobo Books, 1975.

Park Sun-young. "Confucianism Molds Core of the System: Its Legacies Cast Deep Influence." *Koreana* 5, no. 2 (1991): 13-22.

Presidential Commission for Educational Reform. *Korean Educational Reform Toward the 21st Century*. Seoul, 1987.

Price, David. *Between Two Seas: A Journey into South Korea*. Seoul: International Publishing House, 1988.

Rutt, Richard. *Korean Works and Days*. Seoul: Pakmun, 1965.

Seoul National Teachers College. *Bulletin, 1991-1992*. Seoul, 1992.

Smith, Douglas C. *The Confucian Continuum*. New York: Praeger, 1991-1992.

Suh Chung-wha and Kim Tae-kon. *Toward the Improvement of the School Normalization Policy*. Seoul: KEDI, 1985.

"Teaching in America." *Wilson Quarterly* 8 (January 1984): 47-105.

Underwood, Horace G. "Merits and Demerits of Korea Education." *Koreana* 5, no. 2 (1991): 63-69.

Underwood, L.H. *Fifteen Years Among the Top-Knots.* New York: American Tract Society, 1904.

United Nations Educational, Scientific and Cultural Organization (UNESCO). *Proceedings, International Meeting on Education in Bangkok, November 1983.* Bangkok, 1985.

United Nations Educational, Scientific and Cultural Organization (UNESCO). "Report on Education, 1990." Quoted in *Korea Times*, 11 June 1990, p. 1.

ABOUT THE AUTHOR

Douglas C. Smith is a professor and director of the West Virginia University Graduate Center. Smith holds six earned university degrees, including a Ph.D. in history from West Virginia University (1975). In 1993, he also was awarded an honorary Litt.D. for his writing, research, and teaching in the field of comparative education. Since 1977, he has been senior visiting professor of history and languages at a number of Asian universities.

Smith is a Fellow of the Korea Foundation, the Pacific Cultural Foundation of Taiwan, and formerly, Visiting Fellow at Teachers College Columbia University. He is the author of five books, including *The Confucian Continuum* (1992), and numerous articles on comparative education, history, and Asian family life. Smith is a frequent visitor to Asia and currently is working on a project that looks at the impact of westernization and modernization on the traditional Confucian relational system.